MAMBAS

Katie Gillespie

The World of Snakes

www.av2books.com

Step 1
Go to **www.av2books.com**

Step 2
Enter this unique code
AECSDHBIJ

Step 3
Explore your interactive eBook!

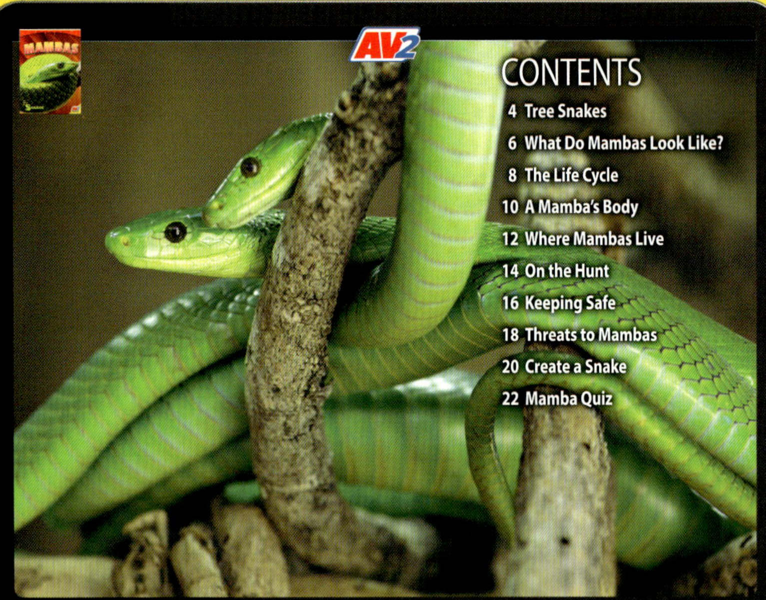

AV2 is optimized for use on any device

Your interactive eBook comes with...

Contents
Browse a live contents page to easily navigate through resources

Audio
Listen to sections of the book read aloud

Videos
Watch informative video clips

Weblinks
Gain additional information for research

Slideshows
View images and captions

Try This!
Complete activities and hands-on experiments

Key Words
Study vocabulary, and complete a matching word activity

Quizzes
Test your knowledge

Share
Share titles within your Learning Management System (LMS) or Library Circulation System

Citation
Create bibliographical references following the Chicago Manual of Style

This title is part of our AV2 digital subscription

1-Year 3–8 Subscription
ISBN 978-1-7911-3306-1

Access hundreds of AV2 titles with our digital subscription.
Sign up for a FREE trial at **www.av2books.com/trial**

MAMBAS

CONTENTS

Tree Snakes

Mambas are some of the world's most feared snakes. There are four different kinds of mambas. One mamba **species** is known as the black mamba. The other three are green mambas. These large snakes are well known for their incredible speed and strong **venom**. Their scientific name comes from the Greek word *dendroaspis*, which means "tree snake."

WARNING

Mambas are often considered some of the deadliest snakes on Earth. A black mamba's **bite** is sometimes called **"the kiss of death."**

Mambas belong to the elapid **family** of venomous snakes. This family also includes cobras and coral snakes. Elapids and all other snakes are reptiles. Reptiles are animals with scales instead of feathers or fur. They breathe air, are **cold-blooded**, and have a skeleton.

SNAKE BITES

Black mambas can reach speeds up to **12 miles** (19 kilometers) per hour.

Venom from a black mamba bite can kill a person in only **20 minutes**.

What Do Mambas Look Like?

A mamba's body is thin and agile. Baby mambas, or hatchlings, are usually up to 24 inches (60 centimeters) long. Adult lengths can vary. Black mambas are the largest mambas. Although they average about 6.6 to 8.2 feet (2 to 2.5 meters), these snakes can grow up to 14 feet (4.3 m) long. They are the longest venomous snakes in Africa.

Measuring Up

Average snake lengths

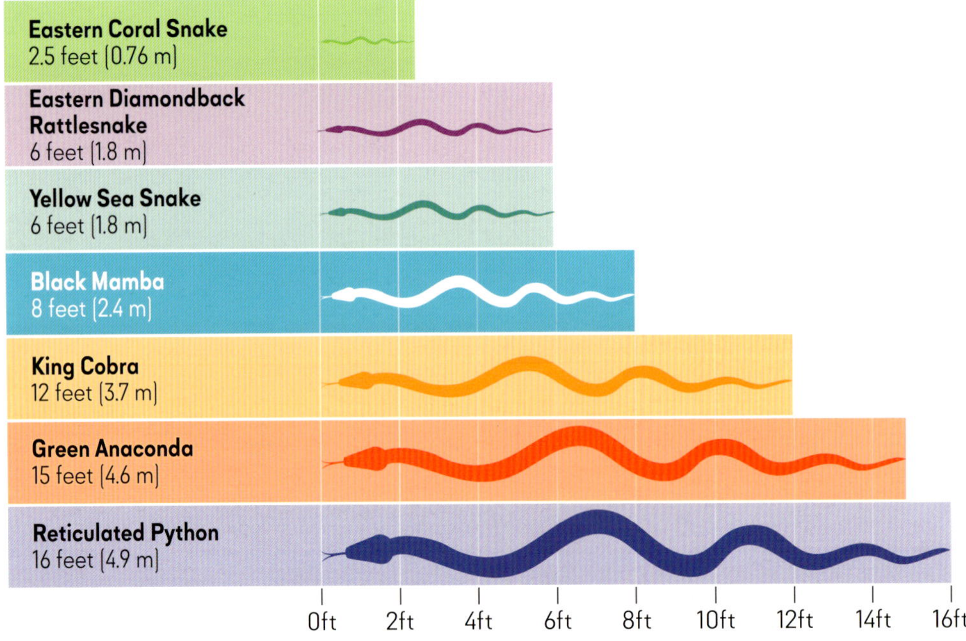

Green mambas are shorter than black mambas. Jameson's mambas range in length from about 4.9 to 6.6 feet (1.5 to 2 m). Eastern green mambas grow about 6 to 7 feet (1.8 to 2.1 m) long. Western green mambas are slightly smaller, at about 4.5 to 6.6 feet (1.4 to 2 m) in length.

A mamba's coloring depends on its age, species, and **habitat**. Adult black mambas are gray, olive, or brown. Jameson's mambas and western green mambas often have dull green scales edged with black. Eastern green mambas are bright green with yellowish green bellies.

The Life Cycle

Like all living things, mambas have a life cycle. A mamba will be born, grow, and **reproduce**. Some mambas live up to 20 years.

1

A mamba mother typically lays between 6 and 17 eggs. The eggs are laid underground or in a hollow tree. They hatch after 2 to 3 months.

2

The mother leaves her eggs to hatch alone. Hatchlings are independent from birth. They absorb **nutrients** from the egg yolk until they are old enough to find **prey**.

3

Young mambas grow quickly. They shed their skin as they grow. Mambas can reach lengths of 6.5 feet (2 m) in their first year.

4

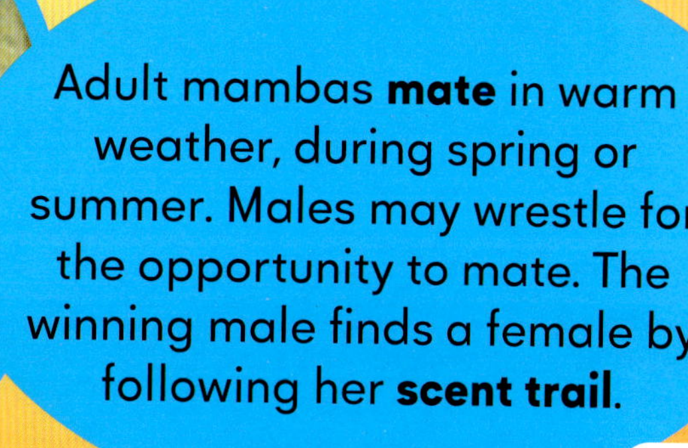

Adult mambas **mate** in warm weather, during spring or summer. Males may wrestle for the opportunity to mate. The winning male finds a female by following her **scent trail**.

A Mamba's Body

Like all living things, a mamba has many different **adaptations**. Some keep the snake safe. Others help it to survive in its habitat.

Scales
A mamba's scales are large and smooth. They grip the ground like hooks to help the snake move forward.

Head
Unlike most snakes, a mamba's head is distinctly flat-sided and shaped like a coffin.

Eyes

Mambas have medium-sized eyes that range in color from grayish brown to black. Their round pupils are ringed in yellow.

Fangs

Mambas have fangs that measure 0.3 inches (6.5 millimeters). They are hollow and can hold up to 20 drops of venom.

Where Mambas Live

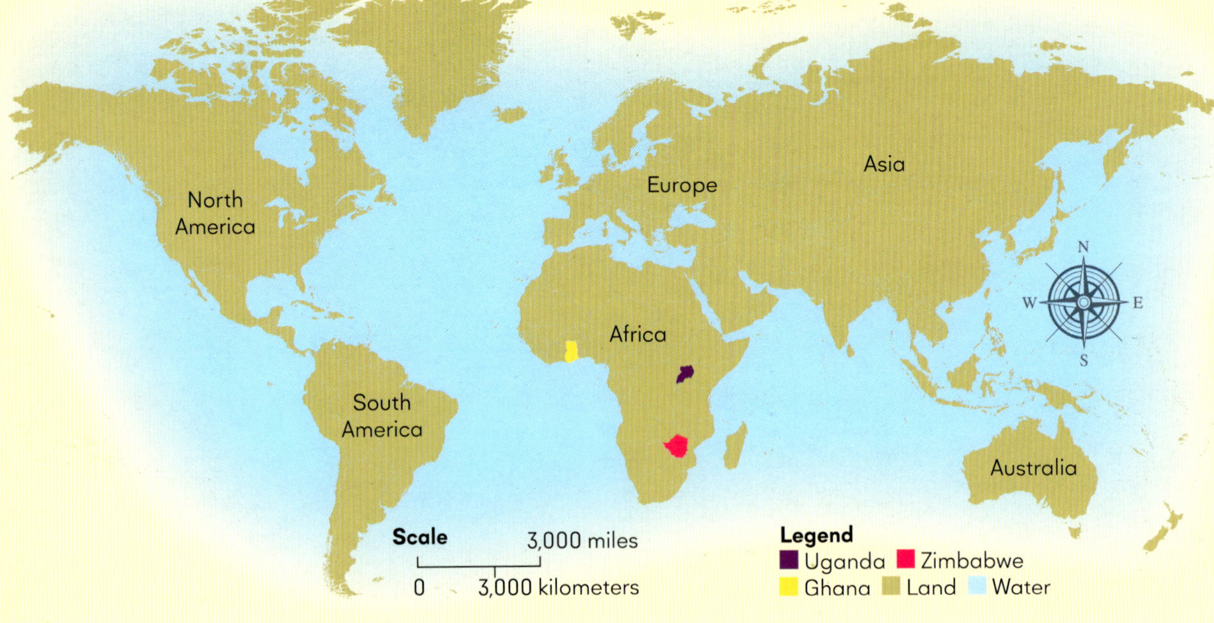

Mambas live in tropical climates. They are native to Africa. Mambas are often found in rainforests, savannas or grasslands, forests or woodlands, and on rocky slopes or mountains.

Mamba Range

Africa

Mamba Habitats

Mountain

Forest

Grassland

Rainforest

Black Mamba

Black mambas have a wide range across **sub-Saharan** Africa, including countries such as Uganda. Unlike other mambas, which are typically **arboreal**, black mambas prefer to dwell on the ground. The inside of a black mamba's mouth is dark black in color. This is where its name comes from.

Eastern Green Mamba

Eastern green mambas are found in east and south African countries such as Zimbabwe. They prefer dry tropical forests and coastal climates. Their green coloring helps them to blend in with the trees they live in. These snakes only move about 18 feet (5.4 m) a day, and may stay in the same place for several days.

Western Green Mamba

Western green mambas live in west African countries such as Ghana. They are often found in environments similar to eastern green mambas. Although they are arboreal, western green mambas also spend time on the ground, especially when hunting. They sleep in trees with dense cover.

On the Hunt

Mambas only need to eat a couple of times a week. They usually hunt during the day, both in trees and on the ground. Their excellent vision helps them detect motion. Mambas prey on a variety of small animals, including birds, bats, mice, rats, squirrels, and lizards.

Unlike other mambas, eastern green mambas hunt by hiding in trees and ambushing animals that pass by.

When it finds prey, a mamba will rise and strike multiple times. It will wait for the animal to die before eating it. Like other snakes, mambas swallow their food whole.

Mambas can digest prey within 8 to 10 hours.

Keeping Safe

Despite their deadly reputation, mambas are not **aggressive**. They are actually quite shy and nervous animals. Mambas will almost always choose to flee when they feel threatened. While a mamba's great speed can aid in hunting, it is more often used to escape tense situations. Their coloring can also help **camouflage** them.

Mambas prefer to avoid confrontation. They will only attack if provoked. In addition to humans, some of their most common **predators** include mongooses, hornbills, cape file snakes, and snake-eagles.

Ground hornbills use their long beaks to hunt mambas while keeping safe from venomous bites.

A mamba may rear up, open its mouth, and flatten part of its neck to scare away threats.

Threats to Mambas

None of the four mamba species are **endangered**. In fact, the International Union for Conservation of Nature (IUCN) classifies black mambas as least concern on its Red List of Threatened Species. This means that mambas are not considered to be at risk of disappearing. However, this may not always be the case. **Deforestation**, human expansion, and habitat destruction are all potential threats to mamba populations.

Black mambas are widespread. This has helped prevent them from becoming threatened.

These activities also increase the risk of contact, which could lead to more mamba attacks on humans, as well as more people killing mambas out of fear. Although they can be dangerous, mambas are a necessary part of the ecosystem. They play a key role in their environment. By preying on small rodents, mambas help to control their populations. It is important to ensure that mamba populations remain stable in the future.

Black mamba and western green mamba populations are considered stable. This means they are not growing or dropping in number.

SNAKE BITES

It only takes **two drops** of black mamba venom to kill a person.

A black mamba will consider humans to be a threat at a distance of **131 feet** (40 m).

ACTIVITY
Create a Snake

There are many different kinds of snakes in the world. They all have certain features in common. However, each snake also has its own unique features. They help the snake live in its home.

Make your own snake by answering the following questions:

1. What is your snake called?
2. Where does it live?
3. What features does it share with other snakes?
4. What features help it live in its home? How do these features do this?
5. What does your snake look like?
6. Use a pencil or pen to draw your snake living in its home. Make sure to include all of its features.

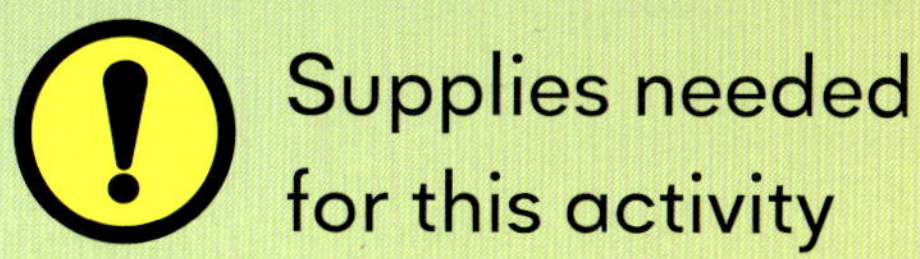
Supplies needed
for this activity

Pencil
or pen
Paper
Eraser

MAMBA QUIZ

How well do you know your mambas? Take this short quiz to find out.

1. How long does it take for a mamba to digest prey?
2. What physical trait helps mambas move forward?
3. How many kinds of mamba are there?
4. On which continent are mambas found?
5. What are some of the mamba's most common predators?
6. Which kind of mamba grows the longest?
7. How much black mamba venom does it take to kill a person?
8. How long does it take for a mamba's eggs to hatch?

ANSWERS

1. 8 to 10 hours **2.** Their scales **3.** Four **4.** Africa **5.** Humans, mongooses, hornbills, cape file snakes, and snake-eagles **6.** Black mamba **7.** Two drops **8.** 2 to 3 months

Key Words

adaptations: changes in animals or plants that make them better able to survive in their homes

aggressive: ready to fight

arboreal: inhabiting trees

camouflage: when an animal blends in with its surroundings so it is not seen by others

cold-blooded: animals whose body temperature depends on if it is hot or cold outside

deforestation: when large groups of trees or forests are cut down to make room for humans to use

endangered: close to becoming extinct

family: a group of living things that share certain characteristics

habitat: the place where a plant or animal lives

mate: come together for breeding

nutrients: substances needed for healthy development and growth

predators: animals that hunt other animals

prey: animals that are hunted by other animals

reproduce: to have babies

scent trail: an odor trail left by an animal for tracking purposes

species: a group of closely related animals or plants

sub-Saharan: the area of Africa south of the Sahara Desert

venom: a toxic chemical produced by some animals

Index

Get the best of both worlds.

AV2 bridges the gap between print and digital.

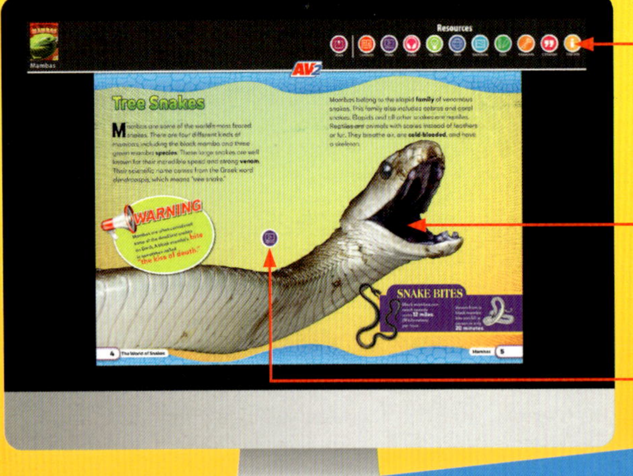

The expandable resources toolbar enables quick access to content including **videos**, **audio**, **activities**, **weblinks**, **slideshows**, **quizzes**, and **key words**.

Animated videos make static images come alive.

Resource icons on each page help readers to further **explore key concepts**.

Published by AV2
276 5th Avenue
Suite 704 #917
New York, NY 10001
Website: www.av2books.com

Library of Congress Control Number: 2021940114

ISBN 978-1-7911-4160-8 (hardcover)
ISBN 978-1-7911-4161-5 (softcover)
ISBN 978-1-7911-4162-2 (multi-user eBook)

Printed in Guangzhou, China
1 2 3 4 5 6 7 8 9 0 25 24 23 22 21

062021
101120

Art Director: Terry Paulhus Project Coordinator: John Willis

Every reasonable effort has been made to trace ownership and to obtain permission to reprint copyright material. The publisher would be pleased to have any errors or omissions brought to its attention so that they may be corrected in subsequent printings.

The publisher acknowledges Alamy, Getty Images, Minden Pictures, and Shutterstock as the primary image suppliers for this title.